Accounting for
Stock-Based Compensation

Steven M. Bragg

AccountingTools®

ISBN 978-1-64221-281-5

For more information about AccountingTools® products, visit our Web site at www.accountingtools.com.

Table of Contents

About the Author

Steven Bragg, CPA, has been the chief financial officer or controller of four companies, as well as a consulting manager at Ernst & Young. He received a master's degree in finance from Bentley College, an MBA from Babson College, and a Bachelor's degree in Economics from the University of Maine. He has been a two-time president of the Colorado Mountain Club, and is an avid alpine skier, mountain biker, and certified master diver. Mr. Bragg resides in Centennial, Colorado. He has written more than 300 books and courses, including *New Controller Guidebook*, *GAAP Guidebook*, and *Payroll Management*.

Steven maintains the accountingtools.com web site, which contains continuing professional education courses, the Accounting Best Practices podcast, and thousands of articles on accounting subjects.

Buy Additional AccountingTools Courses

AccountingTools offers more than 1,500 hours of CPE courses, with concentrations in accounting, auditing, finance, taxation, and ethics. Related courses that you might like include:

- How to Audit Payroll
- Human Resources Guidebook
- Optimal Accounting for Payroll
- Payroll Management

Go to accountingtools.com/cpe to view these additional courses.

AccountingTools®

Accounting for Stock-Based Compensation

Introduction

A company may issue shares to its employees or outside parties that are intended to be compensation for past or future services rendered. These payments can take many forms, such as stock grants, stock options, warrants, and discounted employee stock purchase plans. In this manual, we address how to account for each of these types of stock compensation, as well as similar arrangements. The guidance in this manual applies to all entities.

Overview of Stock Compensation

A company may issue payments to its employees in the form of shares in the business. When these payments are made, the essential accounting is to recognize the cost of the related services as they are received by the company, at their fair value. The offset to this expense recognition is either an increase in an equity or liability account, depending on the nature of the transaction. Employee services are not recognized by the employer before they are received.

Stock Compensation Valuation and Cost Recognition Topics

The following issues relate to the measurement and recognition of stock-based compensation:

Essential Concepts

- *Employee designation.* The accounting for stock compensation noted in this manual only applies to employees, with the exception of the Equity-Based Payments to Non-Employees section. It also applies to the board of directors, as long as they were elected by company shareholders. However, the accounting only applies to stock grants issued in compensation for their services as directors, not for other services provided.
- *Grant date.* The date on which a stock-based award is granted is assumed to be the date when the award is approved under the corporate governance requirements. The grant date can also be considered the date on which an employee initially begins to benefit from or be affected by subsequent changes in the price of a company's stock, as long as subsequent approval of the grant is considered perfunctory.

EXAMPLE

The board of directors of Coronary Associates approves a stock option award to Dr. Jones, who is an employee of Coronary. The board meeting date on which the award is approved is March 15. This is the grant date.

- *Service period.* The service period associated with a stock-based award is considered to be the vesting period, but the facts and circumstances of the arrangement can result in a different service period for the purpose of determining the number of periods over which to accrue compensation expense. This is called the *implicit service period.*

EXPENSE

Mrs. Smith is granted 10,000 stock options by the board of directors of Uncanny Corporation, which vest over 24 months. There is no service specified under the arrangement, so the service period is assumed to be the 24-month vesting period. Thus, the fair value of the award should be recognized ratably over the vesting period.

Costs to be Recognized

- *Expense accrual.* When the service component related to a stock issuance spans several reporting periods, accrue the related service expense based on the probable outcome of the performance condition, with an offsetting credit to equity (usually to the additional paid-in capital account). A performance condition is a condition that affects the determination of the fair value of an award. Thus, always accrue the expense when it is probable that the condition will be achieved. Also, accrue the expense over the initial best estimate of the employee service period, which is usually the service period required in the arrangement related to the stock issuance.

EXAMPLE

The board of directors of Armadillo Industries grants stock options to its president that have a fair value of $80,000, which will vest in the earlier of four years or when the company achieves a 20% market share in a new market that the company wants to enter. Since there is not sufficient historical information about the company's ability to succeed in the new market, the controller elects to set the service period at four years, and accordingly accrues $20,000 of compensation expense in each of the next four years, with an offsetting credit to additional paid-in capital.

If both performance conditions had been required before the stock options would be awarded, and there was no way of determining the probability of achieving the 20% market share condition, the controller would only begin to accrue any compensation expense after it became probable that the market share condition could be achieved. In this latter case, compensation expense would be recognized at once for all of the earlier periods during which no compensation expense had been accrued.

- *Service rendered prior to grant date.* If some or all of the requisite service associated with stock-based compensation occurs prior to the grant date, accrue the compensation expense during these earlier reporting periods, based on the fair value of the award at each reporting date. When the grant date is reached, adjust the compensation accrued to date based on the per-unit fair value assigned on the grant date. Thus, the initial recordation is a best guess of what the eventual fair value will be.
- *Service rendered prior to performance target completion.* An employee may complete the required amount of service prior to the date when the associated performance target has been achieved. If so, recognize the compensation expense when it becomes probable that the target will be achieved. This recognition reflects the service already rendered by the employee.
- *Service not rendered.* If an employee does not render the service required for an award, the employer may then reverse any related amount of compensation expense that had previously been recognized.

EXAMPLE

Uncanny Corporation grants 5,000 restricted stock units (RSUs) to its vice president of sales, with a three-year cliff vesting provision. The fair value of the RSUs on the grant date is $60,000, so the company accrues $20,000 of compensation expense per year for three years.

One week prior to the cliff vesting date, the vice president of sales unexpectedly resigns. Since the award has not yet vested, the company reverses all of the accrued compensation expense.

- *Employee payments.* If an employee pays the issuer an amount in connection with an award, the fair value attributable to employee service is net of the amount paid. For example, if a stock option has a fair value on the grant date of $100, and the recipient pays $20 for the option, the award amount attributable to employee service is $80.

EXAMPLE

Armadillo Industries issues 1,000 shares of common stock to Mr. Jones, the vice president of sales, at a large discount from the market price. On the grant date, the fair value of these shares is $20,000. Mr. Jones pays $1,000 to the company for these shares. Thus, the amount that can be attributed to Mr. Jones' services to the company is $19,000 (calculated as $20,000 fair value - $1,000 payment).

- *Non-compete agreement.* If a share-based award contains a non-compete agreement, the facts and circumstances of the situation may indicate that the non-compete is a significant service condition. If so, accrue the related amount of compensation expense over the period covered by the non-compete agreement.

EXAMPLE

Armadillo Industries grants 200,000 restricted stock units (RSUs) to its chief high-pressure module design engineer, which are vested on the grant date. The fair value of the grant is $500,000, which is triple his compensation for the past year. Under the terms of the arrangement, the RSUs will only be transferred to the engineer ratably over the next five years if he complies with the terms of the non-compete agreement.

Since the RSUs are essentially linked to the non-compete agreement, and the amount of the future payouts are quite large, it is evident that the arrangement is really intended to be compensation for future services yet to be rendered to the company. Consequently, the appropriate accounting treatment is not to recognize the expense at once, but rather to recognize it ratably over the remaining term of the non-compete agreement.

- *Clawback arrangements.* There may be an arrangement under which an employee is required to return shares or profits from the sale of shares. This is called a clawback arrangement, and most commonly occurs as a noncompete mechanism, so that employees will not leave to work for a competitor for a certain period of time. This arrangement is not considered in the grant date fair value of an equity award; instead, it is accounted for only when the contingent event actually occurs. If such a return payment is made, it is recognized as a credit in the income statement, and is limited to the lesser of the compensation cost already recognized for the returned payment, or the fair value of the consideration received.
- *Payroll taxes.* Accrue a liability for the payroll taxes associated with stock-based compensation as of the date of the event that triggered measurement of the compensation.
- *Expired stock options.* If stock option grants expire unused, do not reverse the related amount of compensation expense.
- *Subsequent changes.* If the circumstances later indicate that the number of instruments to be granted has changed, recognize the change in compensation

cost in the period in which the change in estimate occurs. Also, if the initial estimate of the service period turns out to be incorrect, adjust the expense accrual to match the updated estimate.

EXAMPLE

The board of directors of Armadillo Industries initially grants 5,000 stock options to the engineering manager, with a vesting period of four years. The shares are worth $100,000 at the grant date, so the controller plans to recognize $25,000 of compensation expense in each of the next four years. After two years, the board is so pleased with the performance of the engineering manager that they accelerate the vesting schedule to the current date. The controller must therefore accelerate the remaining $50,000 of compensation expense that had not yet been recognized to the current date.

Valuation Concepts

- *Fair value determination.* Stock-based compensation is measured at the fair value of the instruments issued as of the grant date, even though the stock may not be issued until a much later date. The fair value of a stock option is estimated with a valuation method, such as an option-pricing model. See the following Characteristics used as the Basis for Fair Value Determination subsection for more information.
- *Fair value of nonvested shares.* The fair value of a nonvested share is based on its value as though it were vested on the grant date.
- *Fair value of restricted shares.* A restricted share cannot be sold for a certain period of time due to contractual or governmental restrictions. The fair value of a restricted share likely to be less than the fair value of an unrestricted share, since the ability to sell a restricted share is sharply reduced. However, if the shares of the issuer are traded in an active market, restrictions are considered to have little effect on the price at which the shares could be exchanged.
- *Reload valuation.* A compensation instrument may have a reload feature, which automatically grants additional options to an employee once that person exercises existing options that use company shares to pay the exercise price. Do not include the value of the reload feature in the fair value of an award. Instead, measure reload options as separate awards when they are granted.

If the offsetting increase to stock-based compensation is equity, it should be to the paid-in capital account, as noted in the following example.

EXAMPLE

Armadillo Industries issues stock options with 10-year terms to its employees. All of these options vest at the end of four years (known as *cliff vesting*). The company uses a lattice-based valuation model (see the following Fair Value Calculation Alternatives sub-section) to arrive at an option fair value of $15.00. The company grants 100,000 stock options. On the grant date, it assumes that 10% of the options will be forfeited. The exercise price of the options is $25.

Given this information, Armadillo charges $28,125 to expense in each month. The calculation of this compensation expense accrual is:

($15 Option fair value × 100,000 Options × 90% Exercise probability) ÷ 48 Months = $28,125

The monthly journal entry to recognize the compensation expense is:

	Debit	Credit
Compensation expense	28,125	
Additional paid-in capital		28,125

Armadillo is subject to a 35% income tax rate, and expects to have sufficient future taxable income to offset the deferred tax benefits of the share-based compensation arrangements. Accordingly, the company records the following monthly entry to recognize the deferred tax benefit:

	Debit	Credit
Deferred tax asset	9,844	
Deferred tax benefit		9,844

Thus, the net after-tax effect of the monthly compensation expense recognition is $18,281 (calculated as $28,125 compensation expense - $9,844 deferred tax benefit).

At the end of the vesting period, the actual number of forfeitures matches the originally estimated amount, leaving 90,000 options. All of the 90,000 options are exercised once they have vested, which results in the following entry to record the conversion of options to shares:

	Debit	Credit
Cash (90,000 shares × $25/share)	2,250,000	
Additional paid-in capital	1,350,000	
Common stock		3,600,000

Stock Volatility

A key component of the value of a company's stock is its volatility, which is the range over which the price varies over time, or is expected to vary. Since an employee holding a stock option can wait for the highest possible stock price before exercising the option, that person will presumably wait for the stock price to peak before exercising the option. Therefore, a stock that has a history or expectation of high volatility is worth more from the perspective of an option holder than one that has little volatility. The result is that a company with high stock price volatility will likely charge more employee compensation to expense for a given number of shares than a company whose stock experiences low volatility.

> **Tip:** It is useful for a publicly-held company to engage in a high level of investor relations activity in order to manage stock price expectations and thereby reduce the volatility of the stock price. Doing so reduces the cost of stock-based compensation, which is derived in part from the level of price volatility.

Stock price volatility is partially driven by the amount of leverage that a company employs in its financing. Thus, if a business uses a large amount of debt to fund its operations, its profit will fluctuate in a wider range than a business that uses less debt, since the extra debt can be used to generate more sales, but the associated interest expense will reduce net profits if revenues decline.

Characteristics used as the Basis for Fair Value Determination

Fair value is relatively easy to determine when the common stock of a publicly-held company is being issued, since there is an established market price for other shares that are essentially identical to the ones being issued. However, there are many other issuances where this is not the case, or where there are special requirements associated with a prospective stock issuance that can alter its fair value. In these situations, fair value must be derived using a valuation technique that takes into account the following information:

- *Exercise price.* The exercise price of the option.
- *Option term.* The expected term of the option, which is the period during which the option is expected to be outstanding; this takes into account the expected exercise of an option by employees. The expected term of an option is generally shorter than its contractual term, and can be based on historical experience, an analysis of employee ages, lengths of service, and so forth. Another choice is to estimate the term based upon expected future price points of the underlying stock; for example, employees may be much more likely to exercise their options once the market price of the underlying shares exceeds 50% of the exercise price. It is also possible to incorporate published academic research into this estimate, or industry averages. An easier alternative is discussed immediately after these bullet points.
- *Share price.* The price of the shares to be issued.

- *Volatility.* The expected volatility of the price of the shares to be issued, spanning the expected option term. A reasonable way to estimate volatility is the historical pattern of changes in the price of a company's stock, adjusted for anticipated future issues that may impact volatility. If a business has a high debt-equity ratio, the extra fixed cost layer imposed by the debt tends to increase the variability of its earnings, which in turn increases the price volatility of its shares.
- *Dividends.* The expected dividends to be paid on the underlying shares during the expected term of the option. Include the historical pattern of changes in dividend payments in the estimation of future dividends.
- *Interest rate.* The risk-free interest rate during the expected term of the option. Use the implied yield on U.S. Treasury zero-coupon issuances over the term of the option.

A nonpublic entity can make a policy election to apply a practical expedient to estimate the expected option term for all awards having performance or service conditions. This election is available as long as the option is granted at the money, there is a limited time to exercise the award if there is a termination of service, and the employee can only exercise the award (as opposed to selling or hedging it). The practical expedient is as follows:

- If the vesting is dependent on a service condition, set the expected term at the midpoint between the required service period and the contractual term of the award.
- If the vesting is dependent upon the completion of a performance condition, and that condition will probably be achieved, then set the expected term at the midpoint between the required service period and the contractual term of the award.
- If the vesting is dependent upon the completion of a performance condition, and that condition will probably *not* be achieved, then set the expected term at either the contractual term of the award or the midpoint between the required service period and the contractual term of the award (if the required service period is stated).

When developing estimates for these inputs to the valuation model, select the amount that is the most likely; if no value appears to be the most likely, use an average of the range of possible outcomes. The derivation of estimates for these inputs usually begins with historical experience, followed by adjustments to reflect how currently available information indicates how the future might reasonably be expected to vary from the past.

EXAMPLE

Hassle Corporation operates two subsidiaries, one of which is in a long-term, staid industry in which little changes. The other subsidiary is researching and developing quantum computing solutions, which is a wildly fragmented industry where variable profits and market shares are routine. The revenues from the first subsidiary comprise 90% of the company's total sales.

It would be reasonable for Hassle to base much of its expectations for the determination of stock option fair values on the historical experience of the business, since there is a long history of stock price volatility, option exercise behavior, and dividends that can be used. However, if Hassle's board of directors sells off the first subsidiary, the company is left with an entity whose history is wildly variable. In this latter case, it would make little sense to rely upon historical information as the basis for deriving fair value.

Fair Value Calculation Alternatives

When a publicly-held company issues stock compensation, it can derive fair value from the current market price of its stock, which is readily available. This information is not available to a privately-held organization, for which there is no ready market for its stock. The alternative is to estimate share value based on the historical volatility of a related industry sector index, which is comprised of companies that are similar to the entity conducting the measurement in terms of size, leverage, industry, and so forth. This latter approach is called the *calculated value method*. If a nonpublic company operates in several markets, it is permissible to model its stock price volatility on a weighted average of several related industry sector indexes that approximately mirror the structure of the company, or simply rely upon that industry sector that is most representative of its operations. Broad-based market indexes are not acceptable, since they are not sufficiently closely-related to a specific industry.

EXAMPLE

Abbreviated Corporation is a privately-held company that produces short versions of famous literature. The company grants 60,000 stock options to its editorial staff. The company controller elects to use the calculated value method to derive a valuation for the stock options. She locates an industry stock price index for publicly-held publishing companies, from which she derives historical stock price volatility of 27%. She plugs this information and other factors into the Black-Scholes-Merton formula to derive a fair value of $3.18 per share. When multiplied by the 60,000 options granted, the result is total compensation expense of $190,800. Forfeitures are expected to be 20%, so the net compensation expense is $152,640. Since the vesting period of the options is three years, the controller recognizes the net expense at the rate of $50,880 per year, through the vesting period.

When it is not possible to estimate the fair value of an equity instrument, it is permissible to use an alternative valuation technique, as long as it is applied consistently, reflects the key characteristics of the instrument, and is based on accepted standards of financial economic theory. Models that are commonly used to derive fair value are the Black-Scholes-Merton formula and the lattice model. Key characteristics of these models are:

- *Black-Scholes-Merton formula.* Assumes that options are exercised at the end of the arrangement period, and that price volatility, dividends, and interest rates are constant through the term of the option being measured.
- *Monte Carlo simulation.* Uses multiple trial runs on a computer to approximate the probability of certain outcomes, using random variables. This simulation can be run using the Excel electronic spreadsheet.
- *Lattice model.* Can incorporate ongoing changes in price volatility and dividends over successive time periods in the term of an option. The model assumes that at least two price movements are possible in each measured time period.

EXAMPLE

Armadillo Industries grants an option on $25 stock that will expire in 12 months. The exercise price of the option matches the $25 stock price. Management believes there is a 40% chance that the stock price will increase by 25% during the upcoming year, a 40% chance that the price will decline by 10%, and a 20% chance that the price will decline by 50%. The risk-free interest rate is 5%. The steps required to develop a fair value for the stock option using the lattice model are:

1. Chart the estimated stock price variations.
2. Convert the price variations into the future value of options.
3. Discount the options to their present values.

The following lattice model shows the range and probability of stock prices for the upcoming year:

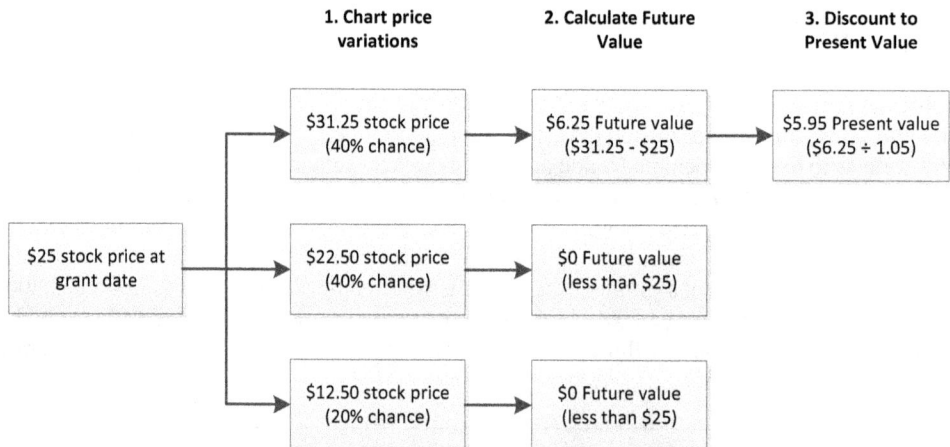

1. Chart price variations	2. Calculate Future Value	3. Discount to Present Value
$31.25 stock price (40% chance)	$6.25 Future value ($31.25 - $25)	$5.95 Present value ($6.25 ÷ 1.05)
$22.50 stock price (40% chance)	$0 Future value (less than $25)	
$12.50 stock price (20% chance)	$0 Future value (less than $25)	

$25 stock price at grant date

In short, the option will expire unexercised unless the stock price increases. Since there is only a 40% chance of the stock price increasing, the present value of the stock option associated with that scenario can be assigned the following expected present value for purposes of assigning a fair value to the option at the grant date:

$$\$5.95 \text{ Option present value} \times 40\% \text{ Probability} = \$2.38 \text{ Option value at grant date}$$

It is acceptable to employ a different valuation model to develop the fair value of different equity instruments. It is also permissible to switch valuation methods if the replacement method can yield a better estimate of fair value. All models must be supportable, in that the assumptions used are fully defensible.

> **Tip:** From an accounting efficiency perspective, it is useful to aggregate individual awards into homogeneous groups for valuation purposes.

Changes in Accounting Estimate

If there is a change in the valuation technique or the method of determining assumptions used in a valuation technique, this is considered a change in accounting estimate. A change in accounting estimate is to be accounted for in the period of change and thereafter. No retrospective change (which is a change to prior-period financial statements) is required or allowed.

Awards Classified as Equity

In this section, we address a number of variations on how to account for awards that are classified as equity arrangements (that is, the offset to compensation expense is an increase in equity). The bulk of these issues relate to subsequent modifications of existing stock-based awards.

Award Measurement Problems

When it is not possible to reasonably estimate the fair value of a stock-based award at its grant date, continue to remeasure the award at each successive reporting date until the award has been settled. Once the award has been settled, adjust the compensation-to-date associated with the award to the intrinsic value of the award. Intrinsic value is the excess amount of the fair value of a share over the exercise price of an underlying stock option.

Award Modifications

An award is considered to have been modified unless *all* of the following conditions apply:

1. The fair value of the modified award is the same as the fair value of the original award.
2. The vesting conditions of the modified award are the same as the conditions that applied to the original award.

3. The classification of the modified award as an equity or liability instrument matches the classification of the original award.

If a stock-based award *is* determined to have been modified, treat the modification as an exchange of the original award for an entirely new award. Thus, the company is assumed to buy back the original award and exchange it for an award of equal or greater value. The accounting for a modified award includes the following points:

- *Fair value basis.* If there is an incremental change in value between the "old" and "new" awards, this is treated as additional compensation expense. The amount of expense is calculated by determining the fair value of the "old" award immediately prior to the terms modification, and subtracting it from the fair value of the modified award.
- *Intrinsic value basis.* If intrinsic value is being used instead of fair value to calculate the associated cost of compensation, measure the incremental change in value by comparing the intrinsic value of the award just prior to modification with the intrinsic value of the modified award.
- *Short-term inducements.* If the company offers short-term inducements to convince employees to accept an alteration of their stock-based compensation plans, only treat these inducements as modifications if they are accepted by employees.
- *Equity restructuring.* If there is an equity restructuring and awards are re-placed with new ones that have the same fair values, do not alter the existing accounting. However, if the fair values have changed, treat the effects of the equity restructuring as a modification.
- *Repurchase of award.* If the company repurchases an award, it should charge the amount of the payment to equity, up to the amount of the fair value of the instruments repurchased. If the amount paid exceeds the fair value of the in-struments repurchased, charge the difference to compensation expense.
- *Cancellation and replacement.* If the company cancels a stock-based award and concurrently grants a replacement award or other form of payment, treat these two events as the modification of terms of the original award.
- *Award cancellation.* If the company cancels an award outright, without any offer to replace the award, accelerate the recognition of any remaining unrec-ognized compensation expense to the cancellation date.

EXAMPLE

Armadillo Industries issues 10,000 stock options to various employees in 20X1. The desig-nated exercise price of the options is $25, and the vesting period is four years. The total fair value of these options is $20,000, which the company charges to expense ratably over four years, which is $5,000 per year.

One year later, the market price of the stock has declined to $15, so the board of directors decides to modify the options to have an exercise price of $15.

Armadillo incurs additional compensation expense of $30,000 for the amount by which the fair value of the modified options exceeds the fair value of the original options as of the date of the modification. The accounting department adds this additional expense to the remaining $15,000 of compensation expense associated with the original stock options, which is a total unrecognized compensation expense of $45,000. The company recognizes this amount ratably over the remaining three years of vesting, which is $15,000 per year.

Income Tax Effects

If there is a compensation cost associated with the issuance of equity instruments that would normally result in a tax deduction at a future date, it is considered a deductible temporary difference for income tax purposes. If some portion of this compensation cost is capitalized into the cost of an asset (such as inventory or a fixed asset), the capitalized cost is considered part of the tax basis of the asset.

If there is a compensation cost that does not result in a tax deduction, do not treat it as a deductible temporary difference. If a future event will change the treatment of such an item to a tax deduction, wait until the future event occurs before treating the item as a tax deduction.

Awards Classified as Liabilities

A key element of stock-based compensation arrangements is whether these arrangements result in an offsetting increase in equity or liabilities. The following situations indicate the presence of a liability, rather than a change in equity:

- *Cash settlement.* An employee can require the issuing company to settle an option by paying in cash or other assets, rather than stock.
- *Indexing.* An award is indexed to some additional factor, such as the market price of a commodity.
- *Puttable shares.* An employee has the right to require the issuing company to repurchase shares at their fair value, where the put feature essentially allows the employee to avoid the risks associated with owning stock.
- *Share classification.* Certain types of share-based payments, such as mandatorily-redeemable shares, are themselves classified as liabilities.

If an award is classified as a liability, the offsetting expense should be remeasured at its fair value as of the end of each reporting period, until the related service has been completed. Any change in value is to be recognized in the measurement period, adjusted for the percentage of required service rendered through the reporting period. Thus, the measurement date for a liability is the settlement date, not the grant date.

If a company is privately-held, management should make a one-time policy decision to either measure the liabilities incurred under share-based payment arrangements at their fair value or their intrinsic value. Further, if the company is unable to estimate the volatility of its share price, the policy decision is to measure the liabilities based on either the calculated value or intrinsic value of the arrangements.

If an award is modified, treat it as the exchange of the "old" award for a "new" award. However, since the accounting for awards classified as liabilities already provides for the ongoing remeasurement of a liability, there is no need for any additional accounting for a modified award.

EXAMPLE

Uncanny Corporation grants 20,000 stock appreciation rights (SARs) to its chief executive officer (CEO). Each SAR entitles the CEO to receive a cash payment that equates to the increase in value of one share of company stock above a baseline value of $25. The award cliff vests after two years. The fair value of each SAR is calculated to be $11.50 as of the grant date. The entry to record the associated amount of compensation expense for the first year, along with the company's deferred tax asset at its 35% income tax rate, is:

	Debit	Credit
Compensation expense	115,000	
Share-based compensation liability		115,000

	Debit	Credit
Deferred tax asset	40,250	
Deferred tax benefit		40,250

At the end of the first year of vesting, the fair value of each SAR has increased to $12.75, so an additional entry is needed to adjust the vested amount of compensation expense and deferred tax asset for the $12,500 incremental increase in the value of the award over the first year (calculated as $1.25 increase in SAR fair value × 20,000 SARs × 0.5 service period).

At end of the vesting period, the fair value of each SAR has increased again, to $13.00, which increases the total two-year vested compensation expense for the CEO to $260,000. Since $127,500 of compensation expense has already been recognized at the end of the first year, the company must recognize an additional $132,500 of compensation expense, along with the related amount of deferred tax asset. When the cash payment is made to the CEO, the entry is:

	Debit	Credit
Share-based compensation liability	260,000	
Cash		260,000

Employee Stock Ownership Plans

An employee stock ownership plan (ESOP) is an employee benefit plan that is designed to invest primarily in the stock of the employer. The essential mechanics of an ESOP are that shares are paid to the ESOP by the employer (there are some variations on the form of payment), which the ESOP retains in a suspense account until it is allowed to allocate them to the accounts of employees. The employees are eventually paid from these accounts as of a later triggering event.

An ESOP is most commonly used to increase employee ownership of a business, but can also be used for the following purposes:

- To fund a 401(k) matching or profit-sharing program
- To replace lost benefits when other retirement plans are terminated
- To give the owners a tax-favorable way to terminate their ownership of the business
- To ward off hostile takeover attempts

The following sub-sections discuss the two types of ESOP, which are leveraged and non-leveraged. Before addressing the specifics of each type of plan, we first make note of two issues that apply to both types of plans, which are:

- *Put options.* If the shares held by an ESOP are not readily tradable, participants in the plan are given put options, which allow them to require the plan to repurchase their shares at fair value. The employer records this buy-back as a purchase of treasury stock.
- *Pension plan reversion.* An ESOP may be created because an employer is terminating a defined benefit pension plan, and wants to avoid the associated excise tax on the plan assets by shifting them into an ESOP. These assets may then be used to either buy employer stock or retire the debt in an existing ESOP. A pension plan reversion usually results in a larger purchase of employer stock than the tax law permits to be allocated to the accounts of employees in a single year, so some of the shares are held in a suspense account until they can be allocated in future years.

Leveraged ESOP

As the name implies, a leveraged ESOP borrows funds in order to buy shares of the employer's stock. The money can be borrowed from the employer, or from an outside lender. If an outside lender is used, the loan is usually guaranteed by the employer. A loan uses the employer's shares as collateral. The following accounting issues relate to a leveraged ESOP:

- *Direct loan financing.* When the employer sponsors a loan from an outside lender to an ESOP (called a direct loan), the employer reports the ESOP's debt obligation as its own debt. The employer must also accrue interest expense on the debt. Further, the employer must report cash paid to the ESOP that is used by the ESOP to service the debt as reductions of the debt and interest payable.
- *Indirect loan financing.* An indirect loan is a loan made by an employer to an ESOP, which is funded by an outside loan from a lender to the employer. The employer should report the outside loan as debt. The employer does not report its loan to the ESOP as an asset, nor does it record any interest income on this loan. Any employer contributions to the ESOP and concurrent debt servicing payments from the ESOP to the employer are not recognized in the financial statements of the employer.

- *Employer loan financing.* An employer loan is a loan made by an employer directly to an ESOP, which is not funded by an outside loan from a lender to the employer. In this case, the employer does not report the loan to the ESOP as an asset, nor does it record any interest income on this loan.
- *Purchase of shares by ESOP.* When an ESOP buys shares from the employer, the employer reports the issuance when it occurs, along with a charge to unearned employee stock ownership plan shares, which is a contra equity account. If the ESOP is using debt to buy shares and buys shares on the open market rather than from the employer, the employer still charges the contra equity account, with the offsetting credit to either cash or debt.
- *Release of leveraged ESOP shares.* Shares held by an ESOP are designated as committed to be released when they will be released by a future scheduled debt service payment and will be allocated to employees for their services rendered in the current period. When shares are committed to be released, the unearned employee stock ownership plan shares account is credited; depending on the purpose of the release activity, the debit may be to the compensation cost, dividends payable, or compensation liabilities account, depending on the situation.
- *Dividends on plan shares.* The tax code allows employers to use the dividends on ESOP shares that have been allocated to participants for debt service, but only if the allocated shares have a fair value not less than the dividend amounts used for debt service. Dividends on unallocated shares that are used to pay debt service are reported by the employer as a reduction of either debt or accrued interest payable. If dividends on unallocated shares are paid to participants or added to their accounts, this is reported by the employer as compensation cost. Dividends on allocated shares are charged by the employer to retained earnings; the related dividend payable can be satisfied either by paying into participant accounts, contributing additional shares, or shifting shares from the suspense account into participant accounts.
- *Direct compensation payments.* If an ESOP is not linked to any other employee benefit or compensation promise, all payments made to the ESOP by the employer are considered to be direct compensation of employees. The employer can recognize as compensation cost the fair value of the shares committed to be released. These shares are typically committed to be released ratably over an accounting period as employees perform their service to the employer, so the average fair value of the shares during this period is used to calculate compensation cost.
- *Debt repayment.* Debt is repaid from employer contributions or dividends to the ESOP. As each repayment is made, shares in suspense are allocated to individual accounts as of the end of the ESOP's fiscal year.

The assistance of independent experts may be needed to estimate the fair value of company shares when determining compensation cost.

Non-Leveraged ESOP

In a non-leveraged ESOP arrangement, the employer contributes either its own shares to the ESOP or cash that is used to purchase company shares. The shares are regularly allocated to the accounts of plan participants based on employee compensation, length of service with the company, or both. The shares are eventually distributed to employees upon their retirement or termination. The following accounting issues relate to a non-leveraged ESOP:

- *Contribution of shares to ESOP*. When the employer makes a contribution to the ESOP, it reports compensation cost in the amount of the contribution.
- *Dividend treatment*. Dividends on shares held by the ESOP are charged to retained earnings.
- *Share allocation*. When the ESOP receives shares from the employer or cash with which to buy shares, the resulting shares are allocated to participant accounts and held by the plan until the shares are distributed to employees at a later date.
- *Compensation cost*. Compensation cost is measured by the employer at the fair value of the shares contributed or committed to the ESOP, or the cash contributed or committed to the ESOP. The assistance of independent experts may be needed to estimate the fair value of company shares when determining compensation cost.

Employee Share Purchase Plans

A company may offer its employees the opportunity to directly purchase shares in the business through an employee share purchase plan (ESPP). These plans frequently offer sales without any brokerage charge, and possibly also at a price somewhat below the market rate.

From an accounting perspective, the main issue with an ESPP is whether it represents a form of compensation to employees. An ESPP is not considered compensatory if it meets all of the following criteria:

- *Employee qualification*. Essentially all employees meeting a limited set of employment qualifications can participate in the plan.
- *Favorable terms*. The terms offered under the plan are no more favorable than those available to investors at large, or does not offer a purchase discount of greater than five percent (which is considered the per-share cost that would otherwise be required to raise funds through a public offering). It is possible to justify a percentage greater than five percent, but the business must reassess the justification on an annual basis.
- *Option features*. The plan only allows a maximum 31-day notice period to enroll in the plan after the share price has been fixed, the share price is based only on the market price on the purchase date, and employees can cancel their participation before the purchase date.

Under the following circumstances, an ESPP is considered to be compensatory, which means that the company must record the difference between the market price of the stock and the lower price at which employees purchase the shares as compensation expense:

- The purchase discount offered under the plan is greater than five percent.
- The purchase price is the lesser of the market price on the grant date or the market price on the purchase date.

EXAMPLE

Armadillo Industries has an employee stock purchase plan, under which employees can purchase shares for a 10% discount from the market price of the company's stock. In the most recent quarter, employees authorized the deduction of $90,000 from their pay, which was used to purchase $100,000 of company stock. Since the discount exceeds the 5% threshold, Armadillo must record the $10,000 discount as compensation expense.

Equity-Based Payments to Non-Employees

An equity-based payment is one in which a business pays a provider of goods or services with its equity, such as shares or warrants. This situation is especially common for a start-up business or rapidly growing company that is trying to conserve cash, and is willing to dilute its equity in pursuit of this goal.

The accounting for equity-based payments depends upon the definition of the recipient, since the accounting for a payment to an employee differs from the accounting when payment is made to anyone else. In this section, we deal with the accounting for equity-based payments to non-employees.

The two main rules for equity-based payments to non-employees are that the grantor must:

- Recognize the fair value of the equity instruments issued or the fair value of the consideration received, whichever can be more reliably measured; and
- Recognize the asset or expense related to the provided goods or services at the same time.

The following additional conditions apply to more specific circumstances:

- *Fully vested equity issued.* If fully vested, nonforfeitable equity instruments are issued, the grantor should recognize the equity on the date of issuance. The offset to this recognition may be a prepaid asset, if the grantee has not yet delivered on its obligations.
- *Option expiration.* If the grantor recognizes an asset or expense based on its issuance of stock options to a grantee, and the grantee does not exercise the options, the grantor does not reverse the asset or expense.

- *Sales incentives.* If sales incentives are paid with equity instruments, measure them at the fair value of the equity instruments or the sales incentive, whichever can be more reliably measured.
- *Equity recipient.* If a business is the recipient of an equity instrument in exchange for goods or services, it should recognize revenue in the normal manner.

The grantor usually recognizes an equity-based payment as of a measurement date. The measurement date is the earlier of:

- The date when the grantee's performance is complete; or
- The date when the grantee's commitment to complete is probable, given the presence of large disincentives related to nonperformance. Note that forfeiture of the equity instrument is not considered a sufficient disincentive to trigger this clause.

It is also possible to reach the measurement date when the grantor issues fully vested, nonforfeitable equity instruments to the grantee, since the grantee does not have an obligation to perform in order to receive payment.

If the grantor issues a fully vested, nonforfeitable equity instrument that can be exercised early if a performance target is reached, the grantor measures the fair value of the instrument at the date of grant. If early exercise is granted, then measure and record the incremental change in fair value as of the date of revision to the terms of the instrument. Also, recognize the cost of the transaction in the same period as if the company had paid cash, instead of using the equity instrument as payment.

EXAMPLE

Armadillo Industries issues fully vested warrants to a grantee. The option agreement contains a provision that the exercise price will be reduced if a project on which the grantee is working is completed to the satisfaction of Armadillo management by a certain date.

In another arrangement, Armadillo issues warrants that vest in five years. The option agreement contains a provision that the vesting period will be reduced to six months if a project on which the grantee is working is accepted by an Armadillo client by a certain date.

In both cases, the company should record the fair value of the instruments when granted, and then adjust the recorded fair values when the remaining provisions of the agreements have been settled.

In rare cases, it may be necessary for the grantor to recognize the cost of an equity payment before the measurement date. If so, measure the fair value of the equity instrument at each successive interim period until the measurement date is reached. If some terms of the equity instrument have not yet been settled during these interim periods (as is the case when the amount of equity paid will vary based on market conditions or counterparty performance), measure the instrument at its lowest aggregate fair value during each interim period, until all terms have been settled.

The grantee must also record payments made to it with equity instruments. The grantee should recognize the fair value of the equity instruments paid using the same rules applied to the grantor. If there is a performance condition, the grantee may have to alter the amount of revenue recognized, once the condition has been settled. The grantee measures the fair value of the equity instruments received as of the earlier of:

- The date when the two parties reach an understanding regarding the amount to be paid and the performance commitment (which is a commitment under which performance is probable because of large disincentives for nonperformance); or
- The date when the grantee's performance is complete.

EXAMPLE

Gatekeeper Corporation operates a private toll road. It contracts with International Bridge Development (IBD) to build a bridge along the toll way. Gatekeeper agrees to pay IBD $10,000,000 for the work, as well as an additional 1,000,000 warrants if the bridge is completed by a certain date. IBD agrees to forfeit $2,000,000 of its fee if the bridge has not been completed by that date. The forfeiture clause is sufficiently large to classify the arrangement as a performance commitment.

Gatekeeper should measure the 1,000,000 warrants at the performance commitment date, which have a fair value of $500,000. Gatekeeper should then charge the $500,000 to expense over the normal course of the bridge construction project, based on milestone and completion payments.

EXAMPLE

Archaic Corporation hires a writer to create a series of books about ancient Greece. The terms of the deal are that Archaic will pay the writer $20,000 and 10,000 warrants per book completed. There is no penalty associated with the writer declining to continue writing books for the series. The writer completes work on the first book in the series on October 31, and then refuses to continue writing books for Archaic.

Archaic should recognize the fair value of the 10,000 warrants associated with the writer's completion of the first book when the writer completes the manuscript on October 31. On that date, the warrants have a fair value of $5,000, so Archaic should recognize a total expense of $25,000, which is comprised of the cash and warrant portions of the payment.

The requirements noted in this section also apply to share-based payment transactions for acquiring goods and services from nonemployees, when the items purchased are to be used in the grantor's own operations. In this situation, the equity instruments issued are measured at their fair value on the grant date, which is the date on which the parties reach a mutual understanding of the key terms and conditions of the award arrangement.

Additional Stock-Based Compensation Concepts

In the following sub-sections, we note several additional issues that are related to stock-based compensation, but which do not easily fit into any of the preceding topics.

Capitalized Compensation

The usual assumption when there are stock-based compensation payments is that there will be an immediate charge to compensation expense. This is not necessarily the case. It is also possible that certain stock-based compensation will be included in a factory overhead cost pool, in which case the compensation will be allocated to the number of units produced in the period; this applied overhead cost will eventually be charged to expense when the units are sold or declared obsolete.

A variation on the concept is that stock-based compensation may qualify to be included in the cost of a fixed asset. This situation can arise if the compensation is associated with the design or construction of an asset, or is meant to subsidize the cost of an asset. If so, the compensation cost will be charged to expense over time, as part of the recurring depreciation charge for the asset.

The Leased Employee

A common employment situation is for a business to lease its employees from a professional employer organization (PEO). The PEO is the legal employer, and provides a range of services to employees (such as human resources counseling), as well as compensation payments and benefits. The lessee business typically makes a periodic bulk payment to the PEO in compensation for these services and expenditures. The preceding discussion of share-based compensation applies to leased employees, but only if all of the following criteria are met:

- The leased person qualifies as a common law employee of the lessee
- The lessor is required to remit payroll taxes to the government on the compensation paid to the leased person for work provided to the lessee
- The lessor and lessee have entered into a written contractual agreement that states the following:
    - The lessee has the exclusive right to grant share-based compensation to the person for services rendered to the lessee
    - The lessee has the right to hire and fire the person, as well as to control his or her activities
    - The lessee has the exclusive right to derive the economic value of the person's services
    - The person can participate in the lessee's benefit plans in the same manner as any other employees of the lessee
    - The lessee agrees to pay the lessor for the compensation and other costs associated with the person

If the preceding criteria cannot be met for an individual and share-based payments are made to that person, then the accounting in the Equity-Based Payments to Non-Employees section applies.

Tandem Awards

A tandem award is an award with at least two components, under which the exercise of one award component cancels the other component. For example, an employee could receive either a stock option or a stock appreciation right that is settled in cash. If the employee elects to take the stock appreciation right with its associated cash payment, then the employer will incur a liability for the compensation. If the employer can instead elect to pay out the award as a stock option, then the compensation instead impacts equity, rather than creating a liability. Thus, a tandem award can result in clear differences in being treated as a liability or equity.

Despite the written terms of a tandem award, it is possible that the historical practices of an employer clearly show that payouts are made in cash. If so, and despite the presence of a settlement option that could be in equity, the award is considered to be a substantive liability.

Dividends Paid on Outstanding Options

An employer may pay employees the dividends on underlying shares while an option is outstanding; that is, the employee is paid dividends without yet owning the associated shares. If employees are not required to return the dividends received if they forfeit their options or similar awards, then the employer recognizes these payments as compensation expense.

Share-Based Awards in an Acquisition

In an acquisition, the acquirer may agree to swap the share-based payment awards granted to employees of the acquiree for payment awards based on the shares of the acquirer. If the acquirer must replace awards made by the acquiree, the fair value of these awards is included in the calculation of the total consideration paid by the acquirer, where the portion attributable to pre-acquisition employee service is considered consideration paid for the acquiree. If the acquirer is not obligated to replace these awards but does so anyways, the cost of the replacement awards is recorded as compensation expense.

Impact on Earnings per Share

If a business is publicly-held, it must report basic and diluted earnings per share information in its financial statements. If there are any stock options or warrants outstanding, these instruments are included in the denominator of the diluted earnings per share calculation, which has the effect of reducing the amount of diluted earnings per share. This is not done when the effect is anti-dilutive, which occurs when a business experiences a loss; in this situation, including the dilutive shares in the calculation would reduce the loss per share.

When an organization has outstanding call options or warrants, their dilutive effects are calculated using the treasury stock method. This method employs the following sequence of assumptions and calculations:

1. Assume that options and warrants are exercised at the beginning of the reporting period. If they were actually exercised later in the reporting period, use the actual date of exercise.
2. The proceeds garnered by the presumed option or warrant exercise are assumed to be used to purchase common stock at the average market price during the reporting period.
3. The difference between the number of shares assumed to have been issued and the number of shares assumed to have been purchased is then added to the denominator of the computation of diluted earnings per share.

In Step 2 of the process, the average market price during a quarterly reporting period is based on the average market prices during all three months of the reporting period. A simple average of weekly or monthly closing market prices is usually sufficient for this calculation. When prices fluctuate considerably, it might instead be necessary to use an average of the high and low prices for the reporting period.

When the year-to-date average pricing is determined, it is based on the year-to-date weighted average number of incremental shares included in each quarterly earnings per share computation.

The treasury stock method will only have a dilutive effect when the average market price of the common stock in the period is greater than the exercise price of the options or warrants.

The following example illustrates the concept

EXAMPLE

Lowry Locomotion earns a net profit of $200,000, and it has 5,000,000 common shares outstanding that sell on the open market for an average of $12 per share. In addition, there are 300,000 options outstanding that can be converted to Lowry's common stock at $10 each.

Lowry's basic earnings per share is $200,000 ÷ 5,000,000 common shares, or $0.0400 per share.

Lowry's controller wants to calculate the amount of diluted earnings per share. To do so, he follows these steps:

1. *Calculate the number of shares that would have been issued at the market price.* Thus, he multiplies the 300,000 options by the average exercise price of $10 to arrive at a total of $3,000,000 paid to exercise the options by their holders.
2. *Divide the amount paid to exercise the options by the market price to determine the number of shares that could be purchased.* Thus, he divides the $3,000,000 paid to exercise the options by the $12 average market price to arrive at 250,000 shares that could have been purchased with the proceeds from the options.

3. *Subtract the number of shares that could have been purchased from the number of options exercised.* Thus, he subtracts the 250,000 shares potentially purchased from the 300,000 options to arrive at a difference of 50,000 shares.

4. *Add the incremental number of shares to the shares already outstanding.* Thus, he adds the 50,000 incremental shares to the existing 5,000,000 to arrive at 5,050,000 diluted shares.

Based on this information, the controller arrives at diluted earnings per share of $0.0396, for which the calculation is:

$$\$200,000 \text{ Net profit} \div 5,050,000 \text{ Common shares}$$

See the author's *Accounting for Earnings per Share* manual for more information about the calculation of earnings per share.

The SEC's View of Stock-Based Compensation

The Securities and Exchange Commission (SEC) has issued a number of comments regarding stock-based compensation in its staff accounting bulletins (SABs). An SAB is a summarization of the views of the SEC staff regarding how GAAP is to be applied. The views stated in an SAB are followed by the staffs of the Office of the Chief Accountant and the Division of Corporate Finance when reviewing the filings of publicly-held companies. For this reason, SABs are closely adhered to by entities registering their securities within the United States. If a publicly-held company does not incorporate the concepts in these bulletins into their financial statements and disclosures, it may receive a comment letter from the SEC.

The following issues related to stock-based compensation have been addressed by the SEC in an SAB. The text is a compressed and clarified version of the full SEC discussion.

* * * * *

Question - Validity of fair value estimation: If a valuation technique or model is used to estimate fair value, to what extent will the SEC staff consider a company's estimates of fair value to be materially misleading because the estimates of fair value do not correspond to the value ultimately realized by the employees who received the share options?

Interpretive response: The staff understands that estimates of fair value of employee share options, while derived from expected value calculations, cannot predict actual future events. If a company makes a good faith fair value estimate in a way that is designed to take into account the assumptions that underlie the instrument's value that marketplace participants would reasonably make, then subsequent future events that affect the instrument's value do not provide meaningful information about the quality of the original fair value estimate. As long as the share options were originally so

24

measured, changes in an employee share option's value, no matter how significant, subsequent to its grant date do not call into question the reasonableness of the grant date fair value estimate.

* * * * *

Question – Preferred valuation techniques: In order to meet the fair value measurement objective, are certain valuation techniques preferred over others?

Interpretive response: There is no GAAP preference for a particular valuation technique or model. In order to meet the fair value measurement objective, a company should select a valuation technique or model that (a) is applied in a manner consistent with the fair value measurement objective and other requirements of GAAP, (b) is based on established principles of financial economic theory and generally applied in that field and (c) reflects all substantive characteristics of the instrument.

The chosen valuation technique or model must meet all three of the requirements stated above. In valuing a particular instrument, certain techniques or models may meet the first and second criteria but may not meet the third criterion because the techniques or models are not designed to reflect certain characteristics contained in the instrument. For example, for a share option in which the exercisability is conditional on a specified increase in the price of the underlying shares, the Black-Scholes-Merton closed-form model would not generally be an appropriate valuation model because, while it meets both the first and second criteria, it is not designed to take into account that type of market condition.

Further, the staff understands that a company may consider multiple techniques or models that meet the fair value measurement objective before making its selection as to the appropriate technique or model. The staff would not object to a company's choice of a technique or model as long as the technique or model meets the fair value measurement objective. For example, a company is not required to use a lattice model simply because that model was the most complex of the models the company considered.

* * * * *

Question – Changing the valuation technique: In subsequent periods, may a company change the valuation technique or model chosen to value instruments with similar characteristics?

Interpretive response: As long as the new technique or model meets the fair value measurement objective just described, the staff would not object to a company changing its valuation technique or model. However, the staff would not expect that a company would frequently switch between valuation techniques or models, particularly in circumstances where there was no significant variation in the form of share-based payments being valued. Disclosure in the footnotes of the basis for any change in technique or model would be appropriate.

*   *   *   *   *

Question – Use of valuation experts: Must every company that issues share options or similar instruments hire an outside third party to assist in determining the fair value of the share options?

Interpretive response: No. However, the valuation of a company's share options or similar instruments should be performed by a person with the requisite expertise.

*   *   *   *   *

Question – Historical volatility considerations: A company is a public entity whose common shares have been publicly traded for over twenty years. What should the company consider if computing historical volatility?

Interpretive response: The following should be considered in the computation of historical volatility:

- *Method of computing historical volatility.* Certain methods used to measure historical volatility may not be appropriate for longer term employee share options if they weight the most recent periods of a company's historical volatility much more heavily than earlier periods. For example, a method that applies a factor to certain historical price intervals to reflect a decay or loss of relevance of that historical information emphasizes the most recent historical periods and thus would likely bias the estimate to this recent history.
- *Amount of historical data.* A company could utilize a period of historical data longer than the expected or contractual option term, if it reasonably believes the additional historical information will improve the estimate.
- *Frequency of price observations.* The staff believes using daily, weekly or monthly price observations may provide a sufficient basis to estimate expected volatility if the history provides enough data points on which to base the estimate. The company should select a consistent point in time within each interval when selecting data points.
- *Consideration of future events.* The staff believes that the company should consider those future events that it reasonably concludes a marketplace participant would also consider in making the estimation. For example, if the company has recently announced a merger with a company that would change its business risk in the future, then it should consider the impact of the merger in estimating the expected volatility if it reasonably believes a marketplace participant would also consider this event.
- *Exclusion of periods of historical data.* In some instances, due to a company's particular business situations, a period of historical volatility data may not be relevant in evaluating expected volatility. In these instances, that period should be disregarded. The staff believes that if the company disregards a period of historical volatility, it should be prepared to support its conclusion

that its historical share price during that previous period is not relevant to estimating expected volatility due to one or more discrete and specific historical events and that similar events are not expected to occur during the expected term of the share option. The staff believes these situations would be rare.

*   *   *   *   *

Question – Other sources of volatility information: What other sources of information should a newer publicly-held company consider in order to estimate the expected volatility of its share price?

Interpretive response: The staff would not object to the company looking to an industry sector index (e.g., NASDAQ Computer Index) that is representative of its industry, and possibly its size, to identify one or more similar entities. Once the company has identified similar entities, it would substitute a measure of the individual volatilities of the similar entities for the expected volatility of its share price as an assumption in its valuation model. Because of the effects of diversification that are present in an industry sector index, the company should not substitute the volatility of an index for the expected volatility of its share price as an assumption in its valuation model.

After similar entities have been identified, the company should continue to consider the volatilities of those entities unless circumstances change such that the identified entities are no longer similar to the company. Until the company has sufficient information available, the staff would not object to it basing its estimate of expected volatility on the volatility of similar entities for those periods for which it does not have sufficient information available. Until the company has either a sufficient amount of historical information regarding the volatility of its share price or other traded financial instruments are available to derive an implied volatility to support an estimate of expected volatility, it should consistently apply a process as described above to estimate expected volatility based on the volatilities of similar entities.

*   *   *   *   *

Question – Homogenous groupings: GAAP indicates that an entity shall aggregate individual awards into relatively homogenous groups with respect to exercise and post-vesting employment termination behaviors for the purpose of determining expected term, regardless of the valuation technique or model used to estimate the fair value. How many groupings are typically considered sufficient?

Interpretive response: As it relates to employee groupings, the staff believes that an entity may generally make a reasonable fair value estimate with as few as one or two groupings.

*   *   *   *   *

Question – Simple methods for estimating expected term: Share options are commonly issued with "plain vanilla" characteristics, which include the following features:

- The share options are granted at-the-money;
- Exercisability is conditional only on performing service through the vesting date;
- If an employee terminates service prior to vesting, the employee would forfeit the share options;
- If an employee terminates service after vesting, the employee would have a limited time to exercise the share options (typically 30-90 days); and
- The share options are nontransferable and nonhedgeable.

As share options with "plain vanilla" characteristics have been granted in significant quantities by many companies in the past, is the staff aware of any "simple" methodologies that can be used to estimate expected term?

Interpretive response: The staff understands that an entity that is unable to rely on its historical exercise data may find that certain alternative information, such as exercise data relating to employees of other companies, is not easily obtainable. As such, some companies may encounter difficulties in making a refined estimate of expected term. Accordingly, if a company concludes that its historical share option exercise experience does not provide a reasonable basis upon which to estimate expected term, the staff will accept the following "simplified" method for "plain vanilla" options consistent with those in the fact set above:

$$\text{Expected term} = ((\text{Vesting term} + \text{Original contractual term}) \div 2)$$

Assuming a ten year original contractual term and graded vesting over four years (25% of the options in each grant vest annually) for the share options in the fact set described above, the resultant expected term would be 6.25 years. Academic research on the exercise of options issued to executives provides some general support for outcomes that would be produced by the application of this method.

Examples of situations in which the staff believes that it may be appropriate to use this simplified method include the following:

- A company does not have sufficient historical exercise data to provide a reasonable basis upon which to estimate expected term due to the limited period of time its equity shares have been publicly traded.
- A company significantly changes the terms of its share option grants or the types of employees that receive share option grants such that its historical exercise data may no longer provide a reasonable basis upon which to estimate expected term.
- A company has or expects to have significant structural changes in its business such that its historical exercise data may no longer provide a reasonable basis upon which to estimate expected term.

The staff understands that a company may have sufficient historical exercise data for some of its share option grants but not for others. In such cases, the staff will accept the use of the simplified method for only some but not all share option grants. The staff also does not believe that it is necessary for a company to consider using a lattice model before it decides that it is eligible to use this simplified method. Further, the staff will not object to the use of this simplified method in periods prior to the time a company's equity shares are traded in a public market.

If a company uses this simplified method, the company should disclose in the notes to its financial statements the use of the method, the reason why the method was used, the types of share option grants for which the method was used if the method was not used for all share option grants, and the periods for which the method was used if the method was not used in all periods. Companies that have sufficient historical share option exercise experience upon which to estimate expected term may not apply this simplified method. In addition, this simplified method is not intended to be applied as a benchmark in evaluating the appropriateness of more refined estimates of expected term.

Also, the staff believes that more detailed external information about exercise behavior will, over time, become readily available to companies. As such, the staff does not expect that such a simplified method would be used for share option grants when more relevant detailed information becomes widely available.

* * * * *

Question – Compensation presentation: A company utilizes both cash and share-based payment arrangements to compensate its employees and nonemployee service providers. The company would like to emphasize in its income statement the amount of its compensation that did not involve a cash outlay. How should the company present in its income statement the non-cash nature of its expense related to share-based payment arrangements?

Interpretive response: The staff believes the company should present the expense related to share-based payment arrangements in the same line or lines as cash compensation paid to the same employees. The staff believes a company could consider disclosing the amount of expense related to share-based payment arrangements included in specific line items in the financial statements. Disclosure of this information might be appropriate in a parenthetical note to the appropriate income statement line items, on the cash flow statement, in the footnotes to the financial statements, or within the management's discussion and analysis section.

Stock-Based Compensation Disclosures

A company that issues stock-based compensation should disclose sufficient information to ensure that users of its financial statements are aware of the nature of these arrangements, the effect of the resulting compensation cost on the income statement, how the fair value of the services received or instruments granted is derived, and the cash flow effects of these arrangements. Disclosure at this level of detail is not required for interim financial statements.

The following disclosures are considered to be the minimum level of information required to meet the preceding disclosure requirements:

- *General description.* The general terms of the arrangements, including service periods, the maximum term of stock options, and the number of shares authorized for awards.
- *Measurement.* The method used to measure compensation cost from these stock-based payment arrangements.
- *Option information.* For the most recent year, the number and weighted-average exercise prices of those stock options at the beginning and end of the year, as well as for those exercisable at year-end, and for those granted, exercised, forfeited, and expired during the year.
- *Fair values.* For the most recent year, the number and weighted-average grant-date fair values of those stock options nonvested at the beginning and end of the year, and for those granted, vested, and forfeited during the year.
- *Multi-year information.* For each year for which an income statement is presented, the weighted-average grant date fair values of stock options granted, the intrinsic value of options exercised, share-based liabilities paid, and the aggregate fair value of shares vested.
- *Vested information.* For stock options that have vested or are expected to vest by the balance sheet date, the number of options outstanding, as well as their weighted-average exercise price, aggregate intrinsic value, and weighted-average remaining option term, stated both for options outstanding and options currently exercisable.
- *Fair value assumptions.* For each year for which an income statement is presented, the method used to estimate fair value, and the assumptions incorporated into these estimations, including expected option terms (which includes expected employee behavior), expected volatility and how it is estimated, expected dividends, the risk-free rate, and the discount for post-vesting restrictions. A privately-held company should also disclose the industry sector index and how it calculates volatility from that index.
- *Compensation cost.* For each year in which an income statement is presented, the aggregate compensation cost recognized that was related to share-based payment arrangements, net of taxes, as well as any amount capitalized. Also, the terms of any modifications and the related change in cost, and the number of employees affected by the modifications.
- *Compensation cost not recognized.* As of the latest balance sheet date, the total cost of compensation related to unvested awards not yet recognized, and the weighted-average period over which this cost will be recognized.
- *Cash receipts.* The cash paid to the company for the exercise of stock options, and the tax benefit realized from the exercised stock options.
- *Cash payments.* The cash paid by the company to settle equity instruments that were granted under share-based compensation arrangements.

- *Policy.* The company policy for issuing shares related to exercised stock options, including the source of the shares (such as treasury stock). If this policy will result in the repurchase of shares in a later period, state the range or estimated amount of shares that will be repurchased.

EXAMPLE

Armadillo Industries discloses the following information about its stock options as part of its year-end financial statements:

The company's 20X2 employee stock option plan permits the granting of stock options to its employees for up to 2,000,000 shares of common stock. All option awards are granted with an exercise price equal to the market price of Armadillo's stock on the grant date. Option awards vest after four years of service and have 10-year terms. All awards issued thus far vest on an accelerated basis if there is a change in control of the company.

The fair values of all option awards are estimated using a lattice-based model that uses as inputs the assumptions noted in the following table:

	20X2	20X1
Expected dividends	2%	0%
Expected term (years)	4.8 – 7.7	4.3 – 7.2
Expected volatility	30% - 55%	35% - 60%
Weighted-average volatility	45%	47%
Risk-free rate	2.3% - 3.0%	2.5% - 3.2%

The expected term of options granted is based on historical experience; expected volatility ranges are based on the implied volatilities of an industry index of stocks; the risk-free rate is based on the U.S. Treasury yield curve on the grant dates.

Option activity under the Armadillo stock option plan as of December 31, 20X2, and changes during that year are noted in the following table:

Options	Shares (000s)	Weighted-Average Exercise Price	Weighted-Average Remaining Contractual Term	Aggregate Intrinsic Value ($000s)
Outstanding at 1/1/X2	985	$18		
Granted	420	25		
Exercised	-570	17		
Expired or forfeited	-120	23		
Outstanding at 12/31/X2	715	20	5.3	$2,860
Exercisable at 12/31/X2	405	18	4.9	$1,620

The weighted-average grant-date fair value of stock options granted during the years 20X2 and 20X1 were $10.15 and $9.68, respectively. The total intrinsic value of options exercised during the years ended 20X2 and 20X1 were $953,000 and $802,000, respectively.

Nonvested share activity as of December 31, 20X2 and changes during that year are noted in the following table:

Nonvested Shares	Shares (000s)	Weighted-Average Grant-Date Fair Value
Nonvested at 1/1/X1	500	$19.80
Granted	75	24.17
Vested	-120	18.25
Forfeited	-20	23.50
Nonvested at 12/31/X2	435	20.52

As of December 31, 20X2, $8,900,000 of compensation cost related to nonvested share-based compensation arrangements had not yet been recognized. We estimate that this cost will be recognized over a weighted-average period of 4.2 years. The total fair value of shares vested in 20X2 and 20X1 was $2,190,000 and $1,990,000, respectively.

A business may choose to disclose additional information that could be useful to the readers of its financial statements, as long as the extra information is reasonable and does not lessen the prominence and credibility of the preceding disclosure requirements.

Equity-Based Payments to Non-Employees

There may be situations where a company issues fully vested, non-forfeitable equity instruments in exchange for goods or services. A likely outcome of this arrangement is that the goods or services have not yet been provided or performed, and so are recorded as a prepaid asset. This prepaid asset should be included within the assets section of the balance sheet, not as a deduction from equity.

An entity that has received an equity instrument should disclose the amount of gross operating revenue attributable to the instrument, since this is a nonmonetary transaction.

Employee Stock Ownership Plans

When an employer sponsors an ESOP, it should disclose the following information:

- *General description.* A description of the plan, the basis by which contributions are determined, and the groups of employees covered. If the plan is leveraged or is a pension plan reversion, note how shares are released and how dividends on allocated and unallocated shares are employed.

- *Policies*. Note all policies followed by the ESOP, such as the method for de-termining compensation, how dividends on plan shares are classified, and how plan shares are treated in the earnings per share calculation.
- *Compensation cost*. The amount of compensation cost recognized in the pe-riod.
- *Share holdings*. The amount of shares held at the balance sheet date, broken down by allocated shares, committed to be released shares, and suspense shares.
- *Fair value*. The fair value of unearned ESOP shares.
- *Repurchase obligations*. The nature of any repurchase obligation, and the fair value of the shares subject to this obligation.
- *Tax benefit*. If there is a material tax benefit related to dividends paid to the ESOP, note its amount and how it is treated in the earnings per share calcula-tion.

Summary

The measurement of stock-based compensation can be complex, but is not inordi-nately so, as long as the accounting staff develops a standard procedure for dealing with these arrangements and follows it consistently. It is also useful to gain the coop-eration of the human resources department in formulating compensation arrangements that consistently include the same terms, so that the pre-existing accounting proce-dures can be readily applied to them. The worst-case scenario is when stock-based compensation plans are issued with substantially different terms, which forces the ac-counting department to adopt unique and detailed accounting plans to deal with each one. In short, a consistently-applied pay system greatly reduces the effort of account-ing for stock-based compensation.

Glossary

C

Cliff vesting. When an employee becomes fully vested as of a specific date, rather than gradually over a period of time.

Committed to be released shares. Shares that will be released by a scheduled debt service payment and then allocated to employees for services rendered to the employer during the current accounting period.

Compensation. The consideration paid in exchange for goods or services.

Contra equity account. An account that is paired with and offsets an equity account.

D

Direct loan. A loan made by a third-party lender to an employee stock ownership plan.

E

Employee. An individual over which a grantor has sufficient control to establish an employer-employee relationship, based on local laws.

Employee stock ownership plan. An employee benefit plan that is designed to invest primarily in the stock of the employer.

Employer loan. A loan made by an employer to an employee stock ownership plan, which is not funded by an outside loan from a lender to the employer.

F

Fair value. The amount at which an asset could be bought or sold in a transaction between willing parties.

G

Grant date. The date on which an employer and employee mutually reach agreement regarding the terms of a share-based payment arrangement.

Grantee. The recipient of stock-based compensation.

Grantor. The issuer of stock-based compensation.

I

Indirect loan. A loan made by an employer to an employee stock ownership plan, which is funded by an outside loan from a lender to the employer.

Intrinsic value. The excess amount of the fair value of a share over the exercise price of an underlying stock option.

M

Measurement date. The date on which the prices and other factors used to measure a share-based compensation cost are fixed.

P

Performance commitment. A commitment under which performance is probable because of large disincentives for nonperformance.

Performance condition. A condition that affects the determination of the fair value of an award.

R

Restricted share. A share that cannot be sold for a certain period of time due to contractual or governmental restrictions.

S

Stock appreciation right. A right to receive a bonus related to the appreciation of a company's shares over a period of time.

Stock option. A contract that gives its holder the right, but not the obligation, to buy shares at a certain price and within a certain date range.

T

Tandem award. An award with at least two components, under which the exercise of one award component cancels the other component.

V

Vesting. The process of earning rights. For example, the passage of time may allow a person to earn the right to a share award.

Volatility. The range over which a price varies over time, or is expected to vary.

W

Warrant. An option to purchase a certain number of a company's shares at a pre-determined price, within a defined time period.

Index

www.ingramcontent.com/pod-product-compliance
Lightning Source LLC
Chambersburg PA
CBHW051427200326
41520CB00023B/7388